STORYTIME STICKERS

The First Christmas

By Lynn Plourde
Illustrated by Julia Woolf

STERLING CHILDREN'S BOOKS and the distinctive Sterling Children's Books
logo are trademarks of Sterling Publishing Co., Inc.

© 2011 by Sterling Publishing Co., Inc.

ISBN 978-1-4027-8187-2

Distributed in Canada by Sterling Publishing
c/o Canadian Manda Group, 165 Dufferin Street
Toronto, Ontario, Canada M6K 3H6
Distributed in the United Kingdom by GMC Distribution Services
Castle Place, 166 High Street, Lewes, East Sussex, England BN7 1XU
Distributed in Australia by Capricorn Link (Australia) Pty. Ltd.
P.O. Box 704, Windsor, NSW 2756, Australia

For information about custom editions, special sales, and premium and corporate purchases, please
contact Sterling Special Sales at 800-805-5489 or specialsales@sterlingpublishing.com.

Manufactured in China
Lot #:
2 4 6 8 10 9 7 5 3 1
06/11

STERLING CHILDREN'S BOOKS
New York

An Imprint of Sterling Publishing
387 Park Avenue South
New York, NY 10016

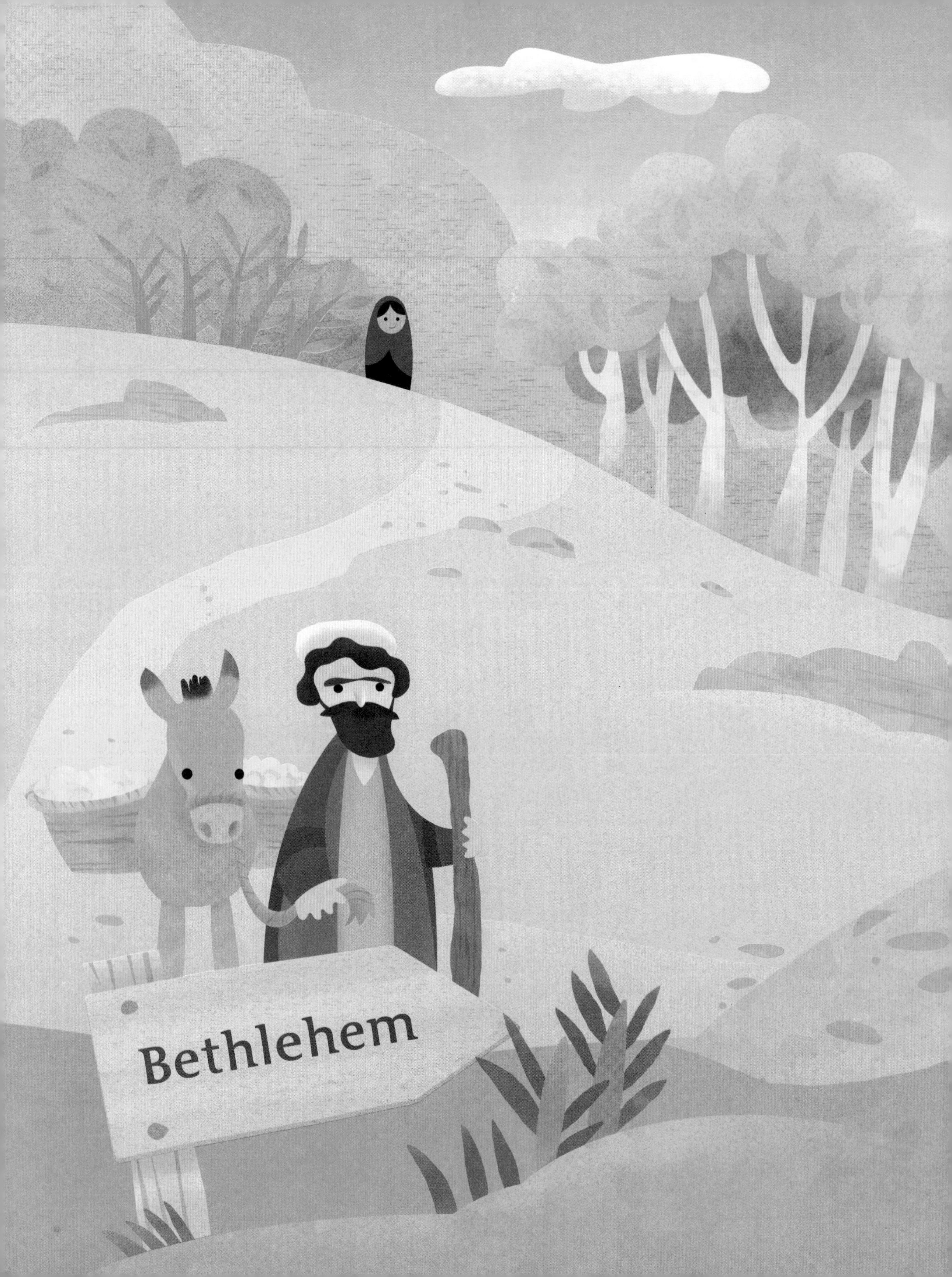
Bethlehem

Joseph led a donkey
for mile after mile.
It carried his wife, Mary,
who was pregnant with child.

INN

They searched Bethlehem
for a room to stay.
But at inn after inn,
they were turned away.

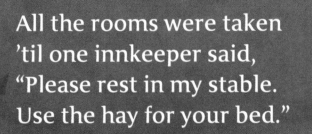

All the rooms were taken
'til one innkeeper said,
"Please rest in my stable.
Use the hay for your bed."

Sheltered with the animals—
baby Jesus was born.
He was laid in a manger
and wrapped to keep warm.

Not far, in a field,
shepherds watched their herd
when a bright star appeared
and an angel gave word.

The shepherds followed the star
to the baby in the straw bed.
They brought a lamb for a gift,
and each man bowed his head.

Three wise men afar
followed that star so bright,
bearing armfuls of riches
to the child born that night.

Baby Jesus was born,
a miracle birth.
Baby Jesus was born,
God's gift to Earth.